The World of
Magic

Peter Eldin

BARRON'S

First edition for the United States, its territories and dependencies and Canada
published in 2001 by Barron's Educational Series, Inc.

Copyright © Haldane Mason Ltd, 2001

All inquiries should be addressed to:
Barron's Educational Series, Inc.
250 Wireless Blvd.
Hauppauge, NY 11788
http://www.barronseduc.com

A HALDANE MASON BOOK
Conceived, designed and produced by Haldane Mason, London, UK
Art Director: Ron Samuel
Editor and picture research: Ambreen Husain
Design: Philip Ford
Artwork: Peter Bull
Color reproduction by CK Litho Ltd, UK

Picture acknowledgments
Aquarius 5, 46; **The Edwin A. Dawes Collection** 7, 10, 12, 14, 16, 18, 20, 24, 26, 28,
30, 32, 34, 36, 38, 40, 42, 44; **Mary Evans Picture Library** 4, 6; **John Fisher** 22.

International Standard Book No.: 0-7641-7504-1

Library of Congress Catalog Card No.: 2001089447

Printed in China

9 8 7 6 5 4 3 2 1

Contents

A History of Mystery

Magic is as old as humankind and is more popular today than ever. Its secrets have survived thousands of years—in spite of books like this one that explain how some of the tricks are done—and magicians continue to amaze and baffle audiences all over the world.

Written records describe magicians performing for the Egyptian pharaohs 5,000 years ago. However, the art of magic goes back many centuries even before that. Down through the ages, numerous performers have entertained audiences with their magical skills.

The early magicians performed on the streets, at markets, and at fairs, going from village to village to entertain the people. The tricks were often very simple, like making coins vanish or producing eggs from a bag. Around 200 years ago, magicians moved into theaters, and many had their own. They also perfomed in private houses and palaces. Their shows and tricks became more and more elaborate and clever.

Crowds would quickly gather around street magicians at markets. Card tricks were always popular, but magicians usually performed a variety of tricks.

The beginning of the twentieth century was a period of really large shows. The magicians would perform big tricks like making a car vanish or a woman float in the air. Often the illusions featured elephants, camels, lions, and other animals.

The invention of television made magic available to more people. As it has universal appeal, magic is popular with audiences all over the world. As a result, more and more people are taking up magic as a hobby, a hobby that is interesting, rewarding, and great fun. Audiences love to be fooled, and magicians will continue to do so until the end of time.

David Copperfield is well known for his spectacular television specials and incredible illusions. Here, he makes a woman float in the air above jets of water.

First Things First

First, a word of warning. Reading this book will not make you a magician! It can tell you how some tricks are done. It can also give you some hints about the best way to present a trick. However, you have to add the interest, the determination, the practice, and your personality to breathe life into the tricks. The great British magician David Devant once said, "To say that a man who can show a few tricks is a magician is as absurd as to say that a man who can recite *The Merchant of Venice* is an actor."

Although lots of magic secrets are in this book, the real secret is to enjoy performing magic and entertaining others.

Magicians use their personalities as well as props to add drama to their tricks.

You can impress with less

Doing one trick well is far better than doing 50 tricks badly. Do not think that you must do all the tricks in this book. Initially, select just two or three tricks you like and practice them. When you are confident that you can do them well, try showing them to friends. Doing a trick in the privacy of your own room and actually performing it in front of an audience are very different.

Practice makes perfect

Even the simplest of tricks should be practiced in private before showing it to anyone. You may need to practice some tricks more than others to get everything right.

The more practice you get, the better you will become. Even professional magicians, who may have performed a trick several times, still make time for practice sessions.

Magic words

During your practice sessions, work out what you are going to say during the trick. Do not leave your words to chance. Work them out first and, if need be, write your words down in a notebook to make sure you get them right every time. Several tricks rely upon the patter (magician's talk) to make them more effective.

All the right moves

Being able to do a trick well is not enough. You must pay attention to detail, to your clothes, and to your movements. What are you going to do with the props after you have finished your trick? How will you walk on and off the stage? How will you use your hands, body, and facial expressions to emphasize different aspects of the performance? All these things have to be thought through.

The Indian magician Sorcar used spectacular sets and special costumes to set the scene for his tricks.

Tricks of the Trade

Watch yourself

Never ever show a trick if you have not practiced it thoroughly in private first. It's a good idea to practice your tricks in front of a mirror so you can see if you are doing everything correctly. An even better idea, if you can manage it, is to videotape your performances so you can watch them from a spectator's viewpoint.

Have you got everything?

Before you think about doing a trick, make sure you have everything you need. Some magicians make checklists so they can be sure that they will not get partway through a performance and then realize they have forgotten something.

Once is magic, twice is dangerous!

Never do a trick more than once for the same audience. People will be fooled the first time and may ask you to do it again. Don't. If you do the trick again, the element of surprise will be gone. The audience will be more likely to work out how you did the trick.

Never reveal your secrets

As you will see from the tricks in this book, the mechanics of magic are often very simple. Do not tell anyone how the tricks are done because people will think that is all there is to it. The mechanics are important, but more important is the way that you present the trick. Giving away the method only tells part of the story and does not account for your hard work in learning and practicing your magic.

Don't be a smarty pants

Don't fall into the trap of trying to prove how clever you are. Just because you know how a trick is done does not make you superior to your audience. You should do magic to entertain, not to belittle, your audience.

Come a Little Closer

Many of the performances by amateur magicians take place not on a stage but with a group of people gathered around the magician. In recent years, magicians have developed this type of magic. Now a lot of professional magicians specialize in what is known as close-up magic. Often in such a situation, the performer and the audience are seated together around a table. This type of magic is more intimate than a stage performance. The magician has to be good with people as many of the tricks involve the active participation of members of the audience.

Companies use close-up magicians at trade fairs and product launches because magic has great drawing power. Close-up magicians are used by some restaurants to provide magic at the tables.

An audience so close is more likely to make comments during the performance. So the magician has to be well rehearsed to cope with such interruptions without destroying the flow of the trick.

The Knot That's Not

You will need:
- *a large handkerchief*

Slydini, who was born Quintino Marucci in Italy, was an expert in close-up magic, baffling even other magicians. When he made coins pass through a solid tabletop, the spectators believed in real magic.

Slydini was particularly noted for his superb misdirection. In its simplest form, this is the art of directing the spectators' attention away from the mechanics of a trick.

One of his best-known tricks simply involved a spectator knotting two handkerchiefs together. No matter how tightly the handkerchiefs were tied, the knots simply melted apart in Slydini's hands. The idea was simple, but when performed by Slydini, this trick became a masterpiece of pure magic.

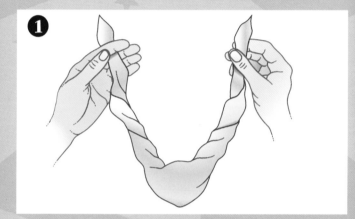

1 *Hold the handkerchief at diagonally opposite corners and twist it between your hands—hold the left corner between the first and second fingers of your left hand and the right corner between the thumb and index finger of your right hand.*

2 *The right hand now puts the right end of the material between the finger and thumb of the left and through the middle fingers.*

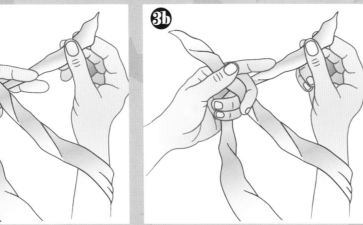

3 Now put your right hand through the loop of material to grasp the original left corner and pull it back through the loop. At the same time, use your left second finger to pull down on the center of the material.

4 As you separate your hands, the material tightens around the small bit retained by your left fingers. Continue to pull until the knot tightens, at which point you can pull out your fingers. Actually, it is not a knot, simply a loop around the middle of the handkerchief.

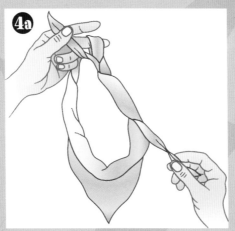

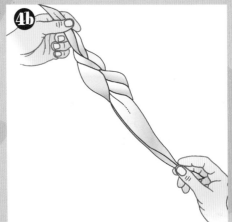

5 Show the spectators the knot between your hands and then blow on it. As you blow, pull your hands apart and the knot will simply dissolve!

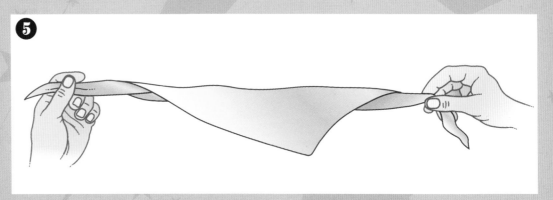

You will need:
- 4 small sponge balls
- 1 large sponge ball

One in the Pocket

New York magician Al Goshman was admired by magicians all over the world for his superb close-up performances. He gave lectures to magicians and told them exactly how he accomplished his tricks—but he still managed to fool them!

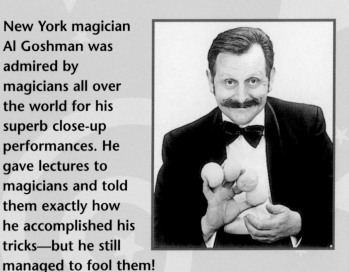

Every so often, Goshman would ask a spectator to lift a saltshaker that rested on the table. Each time the spectator did so, a coin was found beneath the saltshaker—and on each occasion, the coin was bigger than the last.

Today, Al Goshman is best remembered for his work with sponge balls. Many magic dealers still sell sponge balls bearing his name.

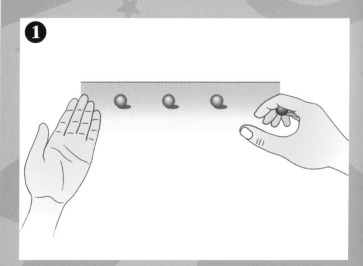

1 The sponge balls can be cut from a piece of foam, or you can buy them from a magic dealer. Alternatively, you could use balls of scrunched-up tissue paper. Place three of the small balls on the table. The fourth ball is hidden in your right hand, held at the base of the second finger. The large ball is in your right-hand jacket pocket.

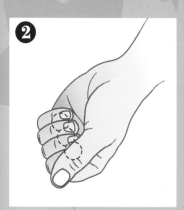

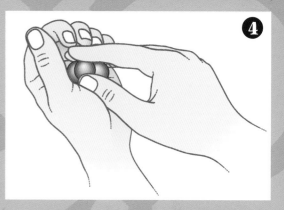

2 Pick up one of the balls with your right thumb and index finger, and drop it into your left hand. Immediately close the left hand. Pick up the second ball, and drop that into your left hand. At the same time, drop the hidden ball from the right hand into the left. Take the third ball, and pretend to place it into your right pocket, actually keeping it concealed in your right hand. To the audience, you apparently have two balls in your left hand. Open the hand and show that you have three.

3 You now appear to take one of the balls from your left hand and place it in your pocket. In fact, what you really do is reach into your left hand, allow the hidden ball to drop from the right, and pick it up again with your fingertips. Place it into your pocket. Once again, you open your hand. Instead of holding the two balls your audience expects, you are holding three again. Allow the balls to roll off your hand and on to the table. As they do this, you remove your right hand from the pocket, holding the large ball at the base of your fingers.

4 Now pick up all three balls and place them in your left hand. Say you will take one. However, unbeknownst to the audience, pick up all three as one and, at the same time, drop the large ball into your left hand. Your right hand returns to the pocket with the three balls held as one and leaves them there.

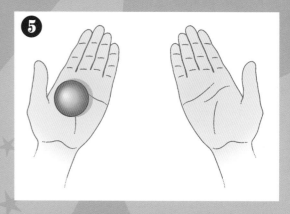

5 All you now have to do is slowly open your left hand to reveal not two small balls, not three small balls, but just one large ball!

Come a Little Closer

You will need:
- *a coin*
- *a bread roll*

There's Money in It

During most of the nineteenth century, German-born Alexander Herrmann was the greatest magician in America and possibly the world. He entertained the royal families of many countries.

Herrmann's show featured many large-scale and elaborate illusions, but he was also extremely skilled at close-up magic. He loved to perform at every opportunity. When he was around anything could happen—and usually did! At a party, someone's ring could easily disappear—only to be found on someone else's finger. He was renowned among grocers in farmers' markets for finding coins inside eggs or fruit. In restaurants, Herrmann found coins in bread rolls—and you can do the same. Not many people carry bread rolls around with them, so this trick is best done during a meal—but don't tell anyone that you are going to do a trick!

1 Secretly hide a coin in your right hand at the base of the two middle fingers. Magicians call this position a finger palm. Take a bread roll in your left hand.

2 Place the roll on top of the concealed coin so you are now holding the roll in both hands, with your thumbs on top and your fingers under the roll. Press down with your thumbs and pull up with your fingers so the roll breaks a little on the bottom, just enough for you to slide the coin into the roll as far as it will go.

3 Break the roll from the top in the normal way —this time your fingers press from under the roll. As the roll breaks across the top, everyone will see the coin in the center of the bread.

Take a Card

Playing cards have been used by magicians ever since they were first invented. They were certainly an important part of a magician's performance by the sixteenth century. One of the earliest recorded performances of a magician using playing cards is that of Francesco Soma from Naples in about 1550. However, playing cards were certainly in use well before that time by the wandering performers who traveled from village to village demonstrating their magical skills.

Even the first English book to explain how magic tricks are done, *The Discoverie of Witchcraft* (tricks were regarded as witchcraft in those days), published in 1584, described "how to accomplish all difficult and strange things wrought with cards."

Many magicians have specialized in card magic. Not all of them have been close-up magicians as you might think. The American illusionist Howard Thurston (1869–1936) began his magical career with a card act. The great escape artist Harry Houdini was once billed as the King of Cards. During the two world wars, a British magician toured theaters with an act consisting solely of magic with cards. He was billed as Billy O'Connor and his 52 assistants. The assistants were, of course, playing cards. However, on one occasion, this caused some confusion when he arrived at a theater to find he had 27 dressing rooms—one for him and 26 for his assistants!

Do as I Do

You will need:
- *1 deck of cards with blue backs*
- *1 deck of cards with red backs*

Canadian-born magician Dai Vernon became interested in magic when he was just six years old! He was regarded as the most influential conjuror of the twentieth century.

Vernon, also known as The Professor, was an important teacher of magic. Fellow magicians and his pupils alike thought him to be the most charming man they had ever met. He mainly did tricks with small objects like balls, coins, and handkerchiefs. However, he was always looking at ways of improving old tricks and creating impressive new ones. During his lifetime, he was regarded as the world's greatest expert on magic with cards.

This card trick is fairly easy to master. Once you get the hang of it, you could soon be the next Dai Vernon!

1 *Allow someone to pick up either deck and shuffle it. You pick up the other deck and give that a good shuffle, too.*

❶

❷

2 *When you have finished shuffling your deck, secretly peek at the bottom card. No one must see you do this. You must remember the card. It is the key card on which the whole trick depends. Hand the spectator your deck, and take theirs. Now ask him or her to do the same as you do.*

3 Spread the cards out in front of you. Take out any card. Do not let anyone see what card you have taken. Look at it and pretend to remember it. (You do not actually take any notice of what card you have taken—you just pretend that you have remembered it.) Place the chosen card face down on top of the deck.

4 Cut the cards two or three times. Swap decks once again. Ask the other person to go through the deck and remove the card he or she remembered, but not show you. You say that you will do the same, but what you really do is look for your key card.

5 Take out the card below it (that will be the spectator's card) and place it face down on the table. The other person puts down the card he or she chose.

6 Turn both cards over. They are exactly the same! It looks as if you have both chosen the same card!

This is Your Card

You will need:
- *a deck of cards*
- *1 double-faced card*

Although a genius at sleight of hand with cards, the Austrian magician Johann Nepomuk Hofzinser (1806–1875) was not above using special gimmicked cards in his performance. He invented numerous methods of conjuring with cards and devised many special cards, some of which are used by magicians to this day.

Hofzinser was a government official in Vienna, but he had a magic room in his home where, three nights a week, he would give performances. He eventually retired from his government job in 1865 to devote himself to magic full-time.

Hofzinser is believed to have invented the double-faced card. Modern magicians use this a lot, and it is used to good effect in this trick.

1   At its simplest, a double-faced card is simply two playing cards glued together back-to-back. Professionally made double-faced cards can also be purchased from magic dealers. Put the double-faced card second from the bottom of the pack. On the bottom of the pack, put the card that matches the upper face of the double-faced card. Replace the pack in its box until you are ready to perform the trick.

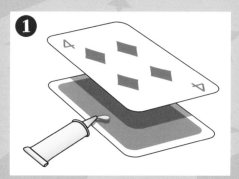

2   To do the trick, remove the cards from their box and place them face down onto the table. Invite a spectator to lift off a portion of the pack and place it to one side.

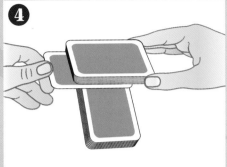

3   Now pick up the original lower portion and place it crosswise on top of the cut-off portion to mark the cut. Leave the pack alone for a few seconds while talking. This will take the spectator's attention away from exactly what you have just done.

4   Now lift up the top half of the pack a little so that you can pull out the bottom card of the top portion. Hand the card to the spectator so he or she can see what card was chosen. Reassemble the pack while the spectator shows the card to everyone else.

5   Now ask the spectator to replace the card anywhere in the face-down pack. To make this easier, spread the cards a little, being careful not to expose the double-faced card on the bottom of the pack.

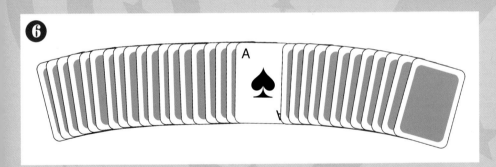

6   You now say that you will make the chosen card turn over. Take the pack behind your back and cut the cards by lifting off a portion from the top and placing it on the bottom (the double-faced card is now somewhere near the center). Bring the cards back in front of you. All you now have to do is ask the spectator for the name of the chosen card. Spread the pack across the tabletop and one card (the double-faced one) is seen face up. It is the card chosen by the spectator!

Think of a Card

You will need:
- *a deck of cards*
- *a secret assistant*

Jean Eugène Robert-Houdin (1805–1871) is often referred to as The Father of Modern Magic. This is because he discarded the heavily draped tables and suspicious-looking clothing of his predecessors, designed modern stage settings, improved existing tricks, and invented new ones. His first public performance was a disaster. Eventually, his new way of presenting magic made him the talk of France.

One of the first of Robert-Houdin's innovations was a second-sight act in which his son Emile would name objects proffered by the audience even though he was securely blindfolded.

Robert-Houdin's second-sight act relied upon an elaborate code memorized by father and son. The following trick also uses a code—but this one is a lot simpler.

1 *Before performing this trick, you and your secret assistant must remember a number up to six digits long. Say that you agree on 534768 (it can be any number you like provided that you can both memorize it).*

2 *Hand someone a pack of cards, Ask the person to pick a dozen or so at random and place them face up on the table while you are out of the room. Add that, during your absence, you want one of the spectators to choose one of the face-up cards.*

3 *When you return to the room, you ask someone (your secret assistant) to point to the cards one by one at random. You stop the person as soon as the chosen card is pointed to (using the number code suggested above, it will be the fifth card).*

4 *A trick like this is more impressive if repeated. Following your number code, this time your assistant makes sure that the third card he or she points to is the selected card. A six-digit code allows you to do this trick six times in a row. If you wanted to, you could go on and on by simply restarting the number sequence. As a rule, do not repeat the trick more than three times —you are there to entertain your audience, not to bore them.*

Time for a Laugh

Most magicians try to inject some humor into their work. Sometimes this takes the form of a few witty comments or even jokes. Often the trick itself or the situation it creates will be funny. David Devant, for example, had his audience in an uproar when he produced eggs because he kept handing them to a young boy who eventually had so many he couldn't hold them. The humor came from the boy's antics as he tried to stop the eggs from falling onto the floor—which they eventually did!

Many magicians have performed purely comic magic, some even going so far as not to be doing any magic at all. Pioneers in the comedy field were Frank Van Hoven and Arthur Carlton Philps. Van Hoven was billed as The Man Who Made Ice Famous because he featured a hilarious sequence that involved a boy trying to keep a grasp on a large block of very slippery ice. In some way, this is a similar idea to the Devant egg trick, the humor coming from the boy's antics. Carlton's billing was The Human Hairpin because, although he was naturally thin and tall, he made himself look funny by wearing a tight-fitting costume, elevated shoes, and a tall, artificial bald head to enhance his gangly appearance.

Fish Supper

You will need:
- *a double bag*
- *a picture of a thin cat*
- *a picture of a fat cat*
- *a cutout paper fish*
- *a cutout paper fish skeleton*

The French comedy magician Mac Ronay, who was born in 1913, has a droll, almost melancholy, approach to magic. He gives the impression that he does not really know what is going on. This, together with his slightly eccentric appearance, makes his act very funny indeed.

Like Mac Ronay, you could adopt a character for your comedy act. Many magicians dress up as clowns and, if you are naturally funny, you could do the same. You might perform your act as a scruffy schoolkid, or a tramp, or a mad scientist carrying out experiments. The choices are endless.

This trick, based on one performed by Mac Ronay, is suitable for most types of comedy act.

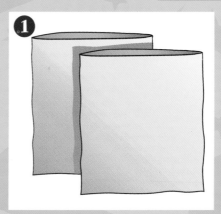

1 To make the double bag required for this trick, simply take two paper bags and glue them together. If you plan to do this trick a lot, make a double bag from cloth because it will last longer.

2 Put the fat cat and the fish skeleton into one of the bag's compartments, and you are ready.

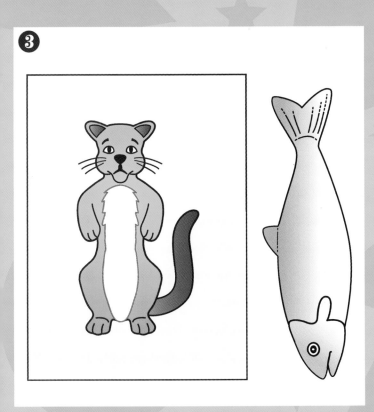

3 During the performance, show the thin cat and the fish to the audience. Place them into the bag (into the empty compartment). This is a simple trick, but its success depends on how it is performed. It's good to have a story to go with the trick. For example, you can make up a story about the cat, or pretend that the hungry cat is chasing the fish over your shoulder, and that the fish is for your supper, not the cat's, so that you can get cross with the cat for wanting to eat the fish. Just see what goes over well with your audience.

4 After a few moments, reach into the bag again (into the other compartment this time), and remove the skeleton fish. Then take out the fat cat—the cat has obviously eaten the fish!

Time for a Laugh

That's Torn It!

You will need:
- *a strip of paper about 2.5in (6cm) x 10in (24cm)*
- *sticky tape*

Carl Ballantine is America's favorite madcap magician. He was born Meyer Kessler in Chicago, Illinois in 1917, and became interested in magic because his barber used to do tricks with thimbles.

Ballantine first performed his comedy act as Count Marakoff, but later changed his stage name to Carl Sharp. In the 1930s, he changed his stage name again, this time to Carl Ballantine and developed into America's leading comedy magician.

During his act, Ballantine performs a version of the Cut and Restored Rope Trick in which a piece of rope is cut into pieces and then restored. At least that is what normally happens with other magicians. However, when Carl Ballantine performs it, the restored rope turns out to be several pieces of rope tied together. The following trick uses a similar idea.

1 First, prepare the paper strip. Fold the strip in half with the short sides touching, and then open it out. Tear the strip into two pieces about 1in (3cm) to the right of the center fold. Now tear the shorter of the two pieces into seven pieces, each about 1in (3cm) long. Stick all the pieces together with tape, and tape the whole lot to the right end of the main strip.

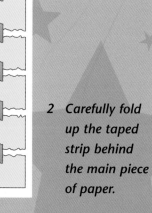

2 Carefully fold up the taped strip behind the main piece of paper.

3 When you do the trick, you show what appears to be an ordinary strip of paper. Your hands hold it at each end so that the folded section, at the rear of the right-hand end, is never seen.

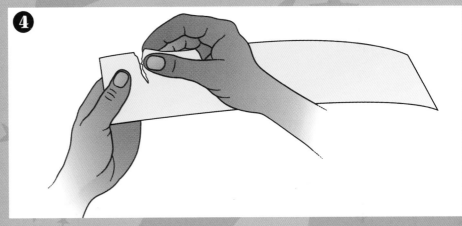

4 Begin tearing the strip into pieces —again about 1in (3cm) long— placing them on top of each other as you do so.

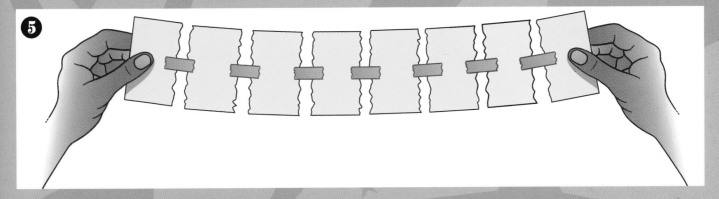

5 Blow on the torn pieces. As you do so, turn the whole lot over in your hands so the taped pieces come to the front. The audience will be expecting you to restore the strip to one piece as that is what magicians do! You now open out the taped pieces (keeping the loose pieces hidden at the back.) You have restored the strip—but not quite as the audience had expected!

You will need:
- *a large handkerchief*

Hair-raising Magic

Even today, many years after his death on stage, Tommy Cooper is revered as Britain's favorite comic performer. His manic laugh, large frame, trademark fez, and tricks that never quite worked out as he anticipated endeared him to audiences. He was a natural visual comedian who had the ability to make people laugh without even doing anything!

The trick that follows is a neat little bit of fun with which you can amuse an audience.

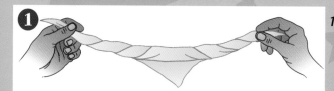

1 Hold the handkerchief at opposite corners and twist it into a rope.

2 Hold the twisted handkerchief in your left hand with your thumb near the center of the rope.

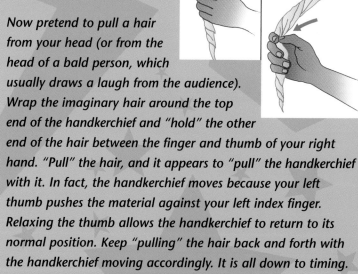

3 Now pretend to pull a hair from your head (or from the head of a bald person, which usually draws a laugh from the audience). Wrap the imaginary hair around the top end of the handkerchief and "hold" the other end of the hair between the finger and thumb of your right hand. "Pull" the hair, and it appears to "pull" the handkerchief with it. In fact, the handkerchief moves because your left thumb pushes the material against your left index finger. Relaxing the thumb allows the handkerchief to return to its normal position. Keep "pulling" the hair back and forth with the handkerchief moving accordingly. It is all down to timing.

On the last "pull", lean forward as if to break the hair with your teeth. Immediately relax your left thumb to allow the handkerchief to move upright once again, and put it away.

Rounding Things Out

When first learning to do magic you should try as many different types of trick as possible. That way, you can find what type of performance suits you best.

As a result, most magicians end up performing a wide variety of different tricks. In fact, many of the greatest magicians in the world do not specialize but, instead, present a variety of magic. Britain's most famous magician, Paul Daniels, is equally comfortable doing close-up magic or large-scale illusions, serious mentalism (mind reading), or comedy, or magic with coins, cards, or whatever else you can think of. Other top magicians who present a variety of effects include David Copperfield and Lance Burton. Both are known for their spectacular illusions but are equally adept at performing small-scale magic at close quarters.

Rounding Things Out

How to Lay Eggs

Isaac Fawkes, also known as Isaac Faux, was born in England in 1675. He was the most successful British fairground magician of the eighteenth century.

Fawkes could often be seen performing his amazing tricks at the Southwark and Bartholomew Fairs and next to the King's Theatre in London. One of his most famous and popular tricks was the Egg and Hen bag—he could produce egg after egg from his magical bag and, for his fantastic finale, he would conjure up a real live hen!

With a little practice, you can transport your audience back to the time of Fawkes and produce enough eggs to make an omelette!

1 Sew one end of the thread to the center of one side of the handkerchief. Use the tape to attach the egg to the other end of the thread. The thread should be just long enough for the egg to hang about halfway down the handkerchief. Put the foam into the bowl.

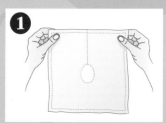

2 Fold the handkerchief in half and lay it on your table alongside the bowl. Put the egg into the bowl. All this preparation is done in secret before you start your performance.

3 Pick up the handkerchief by the two lower corners and hold it out between your hands. The egg remains hidden in the bowl as you show both sides of the handkerchief. Drape the handkerchief over the bowl and wave your hands over it as if casting a spell.

4 Pick up the handkerchief again, holding the top side taut. As you lift it, the egg will be pulled up behind it.

5 Bring both hands toward yourself to fold the handkerchief in half, with the egg hanging inside.

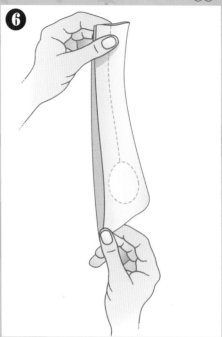

6 Take the two top corners in your left hand and the two bottom corners in your right.

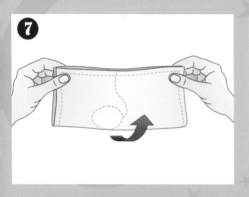

7 Bring your right hand up and lower your left hand toward the bowl. The egg will fall into the bowl.

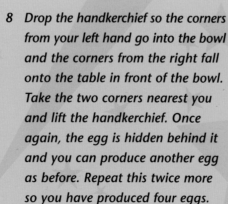

8 Drop the handkerchief so the corners from your left hand go into the bowl and the corners from the right fall onto the table in front of the bowl. Take the two corners nearest you and lift the handkerchief. Once again, the egg is hidden behind it and you can produce another egg as before. Repeat this twice more so you have produced four eggs.

9 Place the handkerchief, with the egg hidden in it, behind another piece of magical apparatus on your table and pick up the bowl. Now pretend to trip. Look as if you have smashed the eggs. Reach inside the bowl and take out the foam—the eggs have become an omelette!

Cups and Balls

You will need:
- 3 cups or beakers
- 4 small, soft balls
- 3 lemons or other small fruits

Matthew Buchinger, who was born in Germany in 1674, was an expert at the classic trick known as the Cups and Balls in spite of the fact that he was born without arms or legs.

The basic idea of the cups and balls, possibly the oldest trick known to magicians, is that balls appear, disappear, move from cup to cup, and may even change their form when placed beneath three cups. An infinite variety of different routines can be used for this trick, with a wide variety of types of cups. Modern magicians tend to use goblets made of spun aluminum that may be purchased from magic dealers, but you can do this trick with almost any type of cup or beaker.

The mechanics of most Cups and Balls routines are quite simple—the real secret is not in any fancy apparatus or complicated sleight of hand, but in the timing and misdirection used. These are elements that come only with practice and experience.

1 *Start with a ball in each cup and the cups, nested together, mouth upward on the table. Put the fourth ball and the three lemons in your right-hand pocket.*

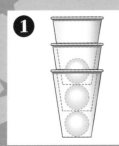

2 *Pick up the cups with your left hand. Take the top cup and, with a quick, swinging movement, place it mouth down on the table. Do the same with the other two cups. The way you move your hand will keep the balls in the cups. Because of the way you have handled them, the audience will assume that the cups are empty. Do not actually say they are empty as that will only arouse suspicion.*

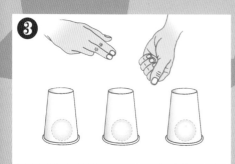

3 Take the small ball from your pocket and pretend to place it in your left hand, actually keeping it in the right. To do this effectively is a matter of timing. Slowly open your left hand over the first cup.

4 With your left hand, pick up the first cup and place its mouth in your right hand. Do not make any great play of this. The reason for picking up the cup is to show that the ball has arrived beneath it. While everyone is looking at the ball, allow the hidden ball from your right hand to fall into the cup. Immediately pick up the ball from the table with your left hand as the right hand returns the cup (with a ball hidden inside) to its former position. Do the same sequence of movements with the second and third cups—the ball vanishes each time and appears beneath a cup. At the end of this sequence, you still have a ball hidden in your right hand. Step back a little as if the trick has now finished, and you may even get a round of applause! At the same moment, place your right and left hands into your pockets.

5 Drop the hidden ball into your right pocket and get hold of one of the lemons. The left hand now lifts the first cup to reveal a ball. Place the cup in your right hand. Pick up the ball with your left hand as the right drops the lemon into the cup and places the cup on the table. Transfer the ball to your right hand, and openly place it in your right pocket.

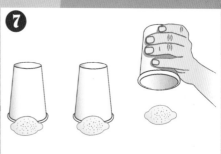

6 Follow the same sequence of movements with the second and third cups so that, at the end, you have a lemon beneath each cup. Again give a slight pause as if the trick has finished.

7 Now lift each cup in quick succession to reveal the three lemons.

An Amazing Production

Chung Ling Soo (1861–1918) had a lavish and spectacular illusion show. However, his biggest illusion was his identity. Although he always spoke through an interpreter, Soo was not Chinese at all but an American by the name of William Ellsworth Robinson. He worked for the great American illusionists Harry Kellar and Alexander Herrmann before adopting his Chinese persona and achieving success for himself.

Soo's performance included many production effects, where a container of some sort is shown empty and then objects are produced from it. One of his tricks used a glass-sided cabinet in which his wife suddenly appeared. She was also produced in an illusion called The Birth of a Pearl in which she appeared in a giant oyster shell that had been shown to be empty. As large oyster shells are not easy to find, here is a production trick that uses some innocent-looking tubes.

You will need:
- *a tube of wood or cardboard with a small window cut out of one side*
- *a colored tube that just fits inside the first tube*
- *a black box that fits inside the second tube*
- *several scarves and/or ribbons and/or flags*

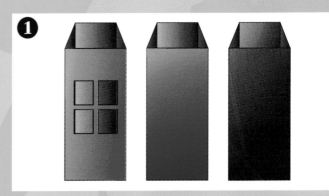

1   The size of the tubes used for this trick depends upon what materials you have available and whether you wish to perform on a small platform or a large stage. A larger apparatus will be required for a stage version, and the size could be big enough to produce a person! Three tubes that nest together are required for this trick. The two outer tubes are painted in bright colors on the outside and matte black on the inside. The innermost container is painted matte black.

2 Although three tubes are used, the audience is aware of only two of them. Put the scarves and other items to be produced inside the black container. Put the second tube over the container and the first tube over that.

❸

3 To perform the trick, you pick up the outer tube and show it to be empty. Replace the outer tube over the second tube (which can be seen through the window of the first tube). Pull out the second tube and show that is empty as well. The cutout section of the first tube seems to allow a view of the interior but this is, in fact, the third inner container. The audience should not, however, be looking at this. They should be watching you demonstrate that the second tube is empty. Replace the second tube.

4 Now, with suitable dramatic effect, reach slowly into the nested tubes and pull out the scarves and other items.

Acting the Part

You will need:
- *2 boomerang shapes cut from card, both the same size (one red, one pale blue)*

Although he died in 1920, David Devant is still often regarded as the best British magical performer of all time. In addition to being a brilliant inventor of both small tricks and large illusions, Devant had an easygoing charm and conversational skills that enhanced his performance and captivated his audience.

In magic, it is not what you do but what the audience thinks you do that is important. Some tricks are accomplished by such simple means that one would think they would never fool anybody. The fact that they work is due to the magician's acting ability. It has been said that a magician is not really a magician, but an actor playing the part of a magician. The following trick must be one of the simplest ever in terms of method, but it will give you a chance to test your acting abilities.

1. *If you hold the blue boomerang above the red one, the red will appear longer. Reverse the positions and the blue will seem to be the longer. It is a simple optical illusion. That is why the success of this trick depends upon the magician's acting ability.*

2. *Show the boomerangs with the blue above the red and say that you have two boomerangs, one of which (the red one) is longer than the other, and will not fit into your carrying case—so you decide to squeeze it shorter. This is where the acting starts, as you "squeeze" the red boomerang to make it shorter.*

3. *Now hold the red boomerang above the blue and something seems to have gone wrong—the red certainly is shorter, but the blue one seems to have grown!*

4. *You decide to try again. This time, however, you work with both boomerangs together, squeezing one and stretching the other. Now you seem to have it right—you hold up the boomerangs (one with its curve up, the other with the curve down), and they are now obviously both the same size!*

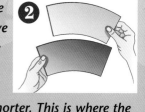

The Specialists

When people take up magic as a hobby, they usually try all types of tricks. This is a good thing because it gives the performer a good all-around knowledge of magic and it also enables him or her to find out what tricks work best. Most magicians continue to present a variety of magic in their acts. Some, however, decide to specialize in just one branch of deception.

The British performer Al Koran presented quite a wide variety of magic but tended to specialize in mental effects. Other British performers who specialized in this area were Maurice Fogel and Chan Canasta. The American magician Ade Duval presented an act consisting solely of magic with silk scarves, and Marvin Roy specializes in tricks and illusions with lightbulbs, including lighting a lighthouse bulb with his bare hands! The French magician Pierre Erdernac does a complete magic act using just rope, and Pierre Brahma, another Frenchman, specializes in magic with jewelry. Probably the most unusual specialist magic act is that of Danish magician Jurgen Samson—the whole act consists of producing loads and loads of tables!

The Specialists

Show Me the Money!

You will need:
- a special coin
- several ordinary coins
- a metal canister

Thomas Nelson Downs (1867–1938) had an amazing ability to manipulate coins. This, combined with a natural charm, soon earned him the title King of Koins. His whole act consisted entirely of magic with coins. People thought that coins would be too small for theater shows, but Downs's act proved very popular. Much of his success was due to his charming personality and superb acting ability.

Although he performed mainly in America, Downs was equally successful in Europe. In 1899, for example, he was booked to appear for just two weeks at the Palace Theater, London, but he was kept on for six months. After that, he signed a five-year contract to appear for 10 weeks every year at the Empire Theatre in London and was the leading performer in continental theaters. One of his most famous tricks was what he called the 'Miser's Dream'. In it, he plucked a seemingly endless supply of coins from the air.

1 You can appear to produce a coin from the air using several different methods. This is one of the simplest as it uses just a coin with a strip of flesh-colored material glued to it.

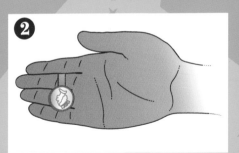

2 Grip the end of the material between the first and second fingers of your right hand (assuming you are right-handed). The back of your hand is toward the audience so they don't see the coin.

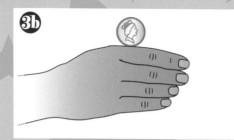

3 Reach into the air and, at the same time, push your thumb up against the coin so it becomes visible to the audience, above the hand, and held by the finger and thumb. It will seem as if the coin has appeared out of thin air!

4 As you do this, pick up, with your left hand, the canister that is lying on your table. Inside the canister are the other coins, overlapping one another a little. You must pick up the canister in such a way that the coins lie beneath your fingers. You now pretend to drop the coin you have just produced into the canister. What you actually do is let go of the coin so it falls back down behind your hand. At the same time your left fingers push off one of the coins in the canister. The audience hears it hit the bottom. Practice this until you get the timing just right. It must seem as if you have dropped a coin from your right hand into the canister.

5 Your right hand now reaches up into the air once again to produce another coin which is again, apparently, dropped into the canister. Keep repeating these actions until all the coins are in the can. For the final coin, actually drop the special coin into the canister as this will leave your hands free for the next trick.

The Great Escaper

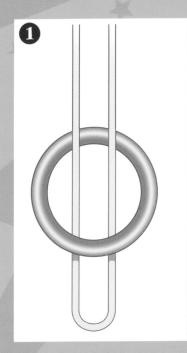

Ask people to name a famous magician and most will come up with the name of Houdini, even though he died way back in 1926. Although born Ehrich Weiss in Hungary in 1874 and taken to America as a baby, Houdini invented his stage name from the name of the great French magician Robert-Houdin.

At first, Houdini performed a wide range of magic. A booking agent persuaded him to specialize in the escapes he featured in his act. From then on, he toured the world escaping from every type of restraint that people could devise. His escapes from a straitjacket while suspended upside down from a high building, and from a packing case thrown into the local river drew crowds wherever he went. He also managed to get out of jails all over the world and from handcuffs brought by people to the theater.

In this trick, a ring, representing Houdini, is tied to a rope, but escapes—by magic.

1 The main secret of the trick is the way that the ring is attached to the rope in the first place. Put the center of the rope through the ring.

2 Now bring the center of the rope up over the sides of the ring and to the top.

3 Pull it tight, and the rope appears to be tied to the ring. Practice these movements until you can do them smoothly and quickly, without looking at your hands.

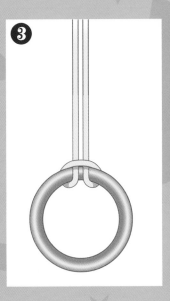

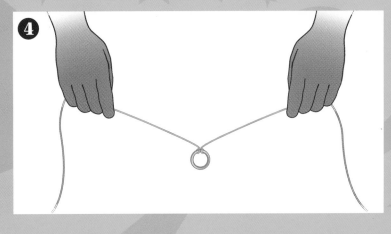

4 Show the ring tied to the rope and ask two spectators to each hold one end of the rope.

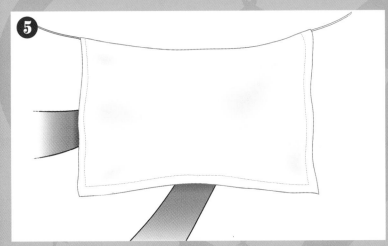

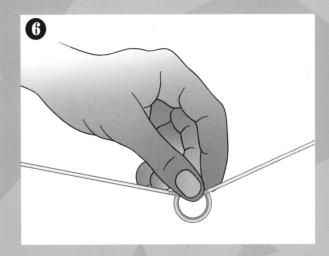

5 Drape the handkerchief over the ring, and place your hands beneath it. You state how impossible it is to get the ring off the rope while the ends of the rope are being held. However, in a matter of seconds, you manage to do just that.

6 In fact, all you have to do is reverse the movements that got the ring onto the rope in the first place.

The Specialists

Man of Mystery

New York magician Joseph Dunninger specialized in mental magic. He convinced radio listeners and television viewers all over America that he could read their minds.

Born in 1892, Dunninger began his career as a boy magician. He owed much of his success to his powerful personality and later to his radio and television broadcasts.

The success of mental magic depends upon the personality and acting ability of the performer. The actual methods used are usually quite simple.

1 To make the special box, you need two boxes, one larger than the other. Cut a large slit in the lid of the large box. Take the smaller box (without a lid) and tape it to the underside of the lid. When you put the lid on the large box, anything put through the slit will go into the hidden box, not the large box. The trick depends on this subtle secret.

2 For this trick, you need to know, in advance, the name of one of the people who will be watching your show. Write that person's name on a dozen or more slips of paper. Put one slip into the envelope and seal it. Place the other slips into the base of the large box. Put the lid on the box.

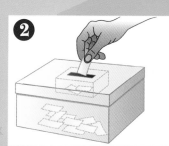

3 During your show, point to the envelope and say that it contains your prediction of something that will happen in the future. Leave the envelope in full view. Hand out slips of paper and pencils and ask each spectator to write his or her name on the slip, fold it in two, and put it through the slit in the box.

4 When this is done, remove the lid and ask someone to pick a slip at random and read out the name (remember—the slips in the large box all bear the same name, while the spectators' slips are hidden in the small box). Then ask someone to open the envelope—inside is a slip bearing the same name!

Masters of Illusion

All magic consists of an illusion. However, to magicians, the word "illusion" usually refers to large-scale tricks that often feature people or animals.

The end of the nineteenth century and the start of the twentieth century was a golden era for big magic shows. By the 1950s, big, spectacular shows were becoming too expensive and eventually disappeared. Then outstanding performers like Doug Henning and David Copperfield came onto the scene, and the big show made a comeback.

Today there are many big illusion shows, particularly in Las Vegas. There you can see Siegfried and Roy who use tigers, and even flamingoes, in their illusions. One of their most baffling and spectacular acts is to make a tiger vanish from a crystal box suspended above the audience. Also in Las Vegas, you can see another American magician, Lance Burton, who can change a pantomime horse into a real live horse! However, the use of animals in illusions is not new. Houdini once caused an elephant on stage to vanish. In the 1990s, Paul Daniels went one better by making an elephant vanish in the middle of an open field! David Copperfield also looked to the past for inspiration when he caused a motorcycle to vanish in midair, an illusion originally performed by the great British magician David Devant in 1913.

One of the first magicians to cause a lady to float in the air was David Devant's partner, John Nevil Maskelyne. Magicians have been causing people and other things to levitate ever since. The American magician John Calvert even had a giant theater organ float around the audience!

Cut in Two

You will need:
- *a specially prepared envelope*
- *a cardboard cutout of a person*
- *scissors*

In 1920, British magician P. T. Selbit stunned the world with a new illusion. A girl was placed into a box that was then sawed in half, but the girl emerged unscathed. At first, it stunned magicians. However, they did not take long to adopt the idea and come up with different versions of the trick.

Horace Goldin's version had the girl's head, hands, and feet extended through holes in the box while it was sawed in half. Later, he dispensed with the box altogether and used a motor-driven buzz saw—an illusion that created a sensation over 30 years later when the Indian magician Sorcar presented it on British television in 1956.

You do not need an assistant or a buzz saw for this miniaturized version of this famous trick.

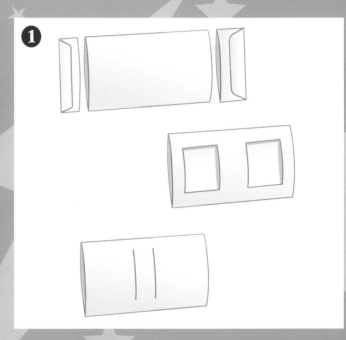

1   Take a long, narrow envelope. Cut off the ends. Make two small windows in the front of the envelope, and two slits in the back as shown. Now seal the envelope so you have a long tube.

2   You can make a cut-out person by sticking a photograph onto an index card and then cutting around it. Alternatively, you can draw a picture of a person onto the index card and then cut it out.

3 To perform the trick, you show the cutout figure and then push it into one end of the tube. It should appear that you simply push the cutout through until the feet emerge at the far end. In fact, you really push the cutout through one of the slits at the back of the envelope and then back in again through the second slit. The central portion of the cutout is now outside the tube but the audience, who can see only the front, is not aware of this.

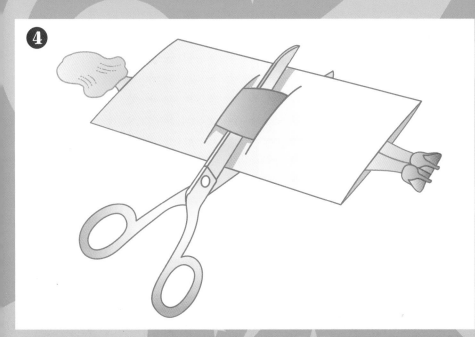

4 Now cut through the center of the tube but secretly insert the scissors underneath the cutout figure, so that they cut between the figure and the tube. Hold both of the cut sections of the tube together as you pull out the cutout person to show that he or she is completely unharmed.

5 It is a good idea to crumple up the tube afterwards. Do this casually, and discard it somewhere safe so that prying eyes do not later discover the secret!

Magic from India

Although India is often depicted as a land of magic, very few Indian magicians have become well-known outside their native land. One exception is P. C. Sorcar (1913–1971),

who toured with a massive illusion show and then took a smaller show to other parts of the world. He billed himself as The World's Greatest Magician. Sorcar was certainly well-known for the amount of publicity he created for himself.

Sorcar's show was lavish, colorful and spectacular, with magnificent stage sets and exotic costumes. The show included the now famous buzz saw illusion, a vanishing motor car, the levitation of a woman, and other big illusions.

Sorcar often performed a large-scale version of the Four Aces Trick, a popular item with magicians that is normally performed close-up. Here is a version of it that you can try.

1 *Remove the four aces from the pack and show them to the audience.*

2 *Place them face down in a row on the table. Put three cards on top of each ace and discard the rest of the pack. Pick up the four packets, one at a time, and put them together.*

44

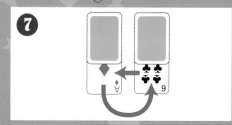

3 From the top of the packet you hold, deal four cards face down, in a row. The fourth card will obviously be an ace—but you ask someone to check. As the ace is turned over, you secretly transfer one card from the top to the bottom of the cards you hold.

4 Now deal the rest of the cards, one at a time, onto the cards on the table so that the cards in the final pile will all be aces. In fact, because of your secret transfer, the fourth pile actually contains one ace and three other cards, and the third pile contains one other card and three aces.

5 Pull out the ace from the bottom of the fourth pile and turn it face up to act as a marker.

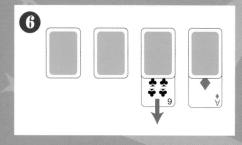

6 The third pile is now chosen by a spectator (see panel), and the other two piles are returned to the pack. The bottom card of the chosen pile is pulled out and turned face up as a marker card.

7 The markers of the two piles are now exchanged. The odd card from the third packet is placed with the fourth (ace) pile, and the ace is moved to the third (chosen) packet.

8 Now turn over all the cards in the fourth pile. The aces have vanished! The cards in the chosen pile are now turned over one by one—they are the aces!

To have a spectator choose pile 3, do the following:

1 Ask a spectator to touch any two piles. If he or she touches 1 and 2, discard them, leaving pile 3 as the chosen pile. If the spectator touches 2 and 3, discard pile 1.

2 Now ask the spectator to push forward one of the piles. If 3 is pushed forward, that is the chosen pile and number 2 is discarded. If the spectator pushes 2 forward, discard it, leaving 3 as the chosen pile. (The same procedure is followed if 1 and 3 are used).

3 So, whatever the spectator does, the magician ensures that pile 3 is the one left on the table.

This procedure is known to magicians as an equivocation force.

Walk Through It

You will need:
- *a long length of rope*
- *an assistant*

David Copperfield is probably the best-known magician in the world today because of his superb magic, spectacular television specials, and some of the incredible illusions he has performed. These include making the Statue of Liberty disappear, and walking through the Great Wall of China!

Many magicians have featured walking through objects in their acts. C. A. Alexander, who specialized in mental magic, walked through a wall of ice in Alaska. Houdini made a feature of walking through a brick wall that had been erected on stage.

On a smaller scale, numerous magicians have performed walking through a ribbon or a rope. Here's a version you can try.

1 *Two spectators are invited on stage to assist. They stand on either side of the stage. Your assistant hands each of them one end of the rope to hold. The rope is stretched across the stage with you standing behind it.*

2 *Your assistant now walks behind you and gets one end of the rope from one spectator. The assistant then walks to the other side of the stage (going behind you in the process to get the other end of the rope).*

3 *Your assistant now takes the rope behind your back and ties it tightly around you. At least that is what appears to happen. In actual fact, you stick up your thumbs behind your back, and the rope is merely looped around them in the pretence of tying one or more knots. Make sure that the looping is done exactly as shown in the picture or you could end up breaking your thumbs. If you want to, the rope could now be brought around to the front of your body and tied together (really tied this time).*

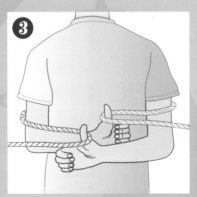

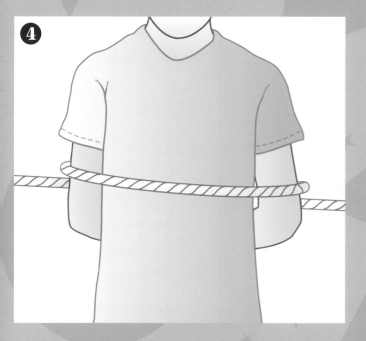

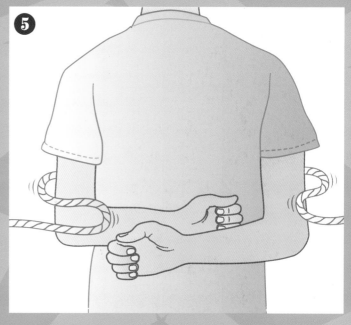

4   The ends of the rope are now handed back to the two spectators. You are apparently securely tied in the middle.

5   You now appear to melt through the rope, but all you really do is lower your thumbs and take a step backward. The rope falls free as it apparently penetrates your body.

Index